Chris Bainbridge is a Bury-based poet a
performing on the North West scene sinc
been writing since his teens back in the 1.
of his working life in health and social care ..ecently
for the Stroke Association. He has also had ...ns as a factory
labourer, ambulance driver, customs officer, disc jockey, and by
accident for one night only, roadie for rock icons Motorhead.

Chris has spoken at numerous events including two national
demonstrations for CND at Aldermaston. He compared the popular
Raise The Roof music festival in 2014, and for five consecutive
years has been the only non-music act to perform at the Glaston-
BURY festival in his home town. Chris has recently facilitated writing
workshops with groups of stroke survivors, and gave a presentation
of poetry at the 2016 conference for World Stroke Day at Fairfield
Hospital.

Now a grandfather, Chris's poetry reflects his varied life and work
experiences as well as his passion for social and political change.

Many thanks to Coreen Cottam for the use of her beautiful painting
"Coming Home" on the back cover and on page 24 I am grateful to
so many wonderful people, particularly family members, close
friends, colleagues and comrades. Without their support and endless
inspiration this book would not have been possible

Best Wishes

Chris Bainbridge

13.12.16

1

Printed in the UK for Reading Room Café Project Publishing 2016

A Poet Who Does Covers

Like the unrequited tragedy of scores of star-crossed lovers,
nothing is as painful as a poet who does covers.

I fell in love with an alien being to the north of Katmandu,
Awake! I would have liked you to have been deep-frozen too,
I wandered lonely as a cloud and pondered many times
the lie that words of other men may make our lives sublime.

If music be the food of love, play on, so said the bard,
and if you play an instrument it isn't very hard
To crash through some back-catalogue of melodies to share,
you didn't write the bloody thing, but no-one seems to care.

But poetry? That's different. Somehow it's not felt cool
to use the words of others, break the last unwritten rule,
The dreams you share in public must be yours and yours alone,
better find yourself a message and some words to call your own
and take them home.

Like the unrequited tragedy of squads of star-crossed lovers,
nothing is a painful as a poet who does covers,
A curse on all their verses and their misbegotten mothers,
a special pit of hell awaits a poet who does covers.

Animals

Gorged on your summer fruits
replete with ripe-skinned,
Flame-headed bounty
I am filled with your sun;
So radiant in your glow
I fear no cold and want the winter.
A cooling cave awaits
where fierce passions hibernate
And I curl up, conserve,
renew, recover, reserve
And lick my wounds
as well as yours;
This hypnotic pause
for contemplation, contrast, content,
I lie and don't repent
only temporarily spent
For the seasons like our love
will not relent.
And as the solstice fires roar
my flesh and spirit then restored
We look to spring
and make our summer's heat
once more.

Aquarius

The world is fouled by fascism, abuse and villains various,
governments of greed with all their practices nefarious,
The suffering of innocents the rulers find hilarious,
my anger's grown to fever-pitch, malevolent, malarious,
my friends, this is the ageing of the Dawn of Aqaurius…

In tolerance and empathy our forbears taught us well,
justice, truth, morality should cast a lasting spell,
But all the Tories care for is the shit they buy and sell,
we need to smash some windows just to get rid of the smell,
and if I had the chance I swear I'd send them all to hell.

So just switch off the telly, turn your back on thrills vicarious,
real life is with your fellow folk, by nature quite gregarious,
It's when we get together that the bosses find us scariest,
we can see they're on the fiddle, I'm not talking Stradivarius,
They'll play a different tune when the worm has turned contrarius,
their bony fingers' grasp of power is what I call precarious,
We'll dance all night and morning in the Age of Aquarius,
we'll see once more the dawning of the Age of Aquarius.

Away

Away with your texts and greetings cards,
poor excuses for being far apart,
Persuading us to humbly accept

the ongoing disaster of our diaspora.
To travel can bring adventure
but should be no obligation,
Dispersal of loved ones or entire nations
seen as inevitable.
We shrug and sigh, and phone and skype.

It would be nice to have a home,
decide for ourselves whether or not to roam
wide and far, or have the chance to stay
just where we already are.

I want my journeys – sometimes – to end.
To bond with family and friends,
kick off my boots, put down some roots,
stake my claim to a place, as well as a name.
Wage slavery nor property-market fluctuation
should force us not to remain.

Let's build simple shelters
and all come home again.

Caravan

It was hot in Essex in 1965. I was six.

We scrambled to shade, in wooded glades we played
fleeing from intense sunshine and other phenomena

unknown to our Geordie sensibilities –
Squadrons of kamikaze wasps,
unphazed by our anti air-raid newspapers,
if the fly-killer ran out they were laquered
by Bellair.

Massive black slugs like fat sidewalk serpents,
so numerous it was a challenge to Tiptree tiptoe
around them.
And my ears filled with exotic new sounds,
the southern natives and the Irish traveller kids
we palled around with,
Mary Morrison and her little brood.

Sounds from even further away
courtesy of Radio London, "the Big L",
Sonny and Cher from Californ–I-ay,
me and big Sis singing "I got you, Babe",
We're on the same medium wavelength,
Our transistorised telepathy, sibling symmetry, symbiosis.
I got you alright, we always got each other.
"Put your little hand in mine",
I cry when I hear it, every time.

While Dad worked on the building-site
we played morning, noon and night
and stayed in a caravan, cosy, even cramped,
but it was An Adventure!

Mam got busy with the pan as was ever her way,

smokey bacon every day.
The pig farm down the road had its drawbacks too,
but at least gave perspective to our chemical loo…
And all too soon we withdrew.
The summer went quickly, as they continue to do,
and innocence and youth began to retreat
as bricks and roads came to replace hedges and fields,
the very grass beneath our barefoot feet.
One last roll of pennies at the village fete,
one more ice cream for the fate of the village.

Our happy hiatus
in the progress of pillage.

Children In Need

Children in need, children in need,
the system is built upon corporate greed,
Where rich men put trademarks on plants and their seeds
and a baby can die for the want of a feed
or a cheap, magic drug in her handful of rice,
Where they bottle the rainfall and slap on a price
and beggar thy neighbour's the only advice,
Where for one to succeed a million must fail
and innocents suffer while monsters prevail,
Collateral damage a price they all pay
to shore up a system where tyrants hold sway.

But just now and then, if the cameras are on,
they put on a show with a dance and a song,
Pop stars and celebrities queue at the doors
to lend their support to this wonderful cause,
"It's Children In Need, man – CHILDREN IN NEED!"
Dress up like a dick and forget all the greed,
The stars all come out and we fill up their tins,
they're so glad they're not cursed with original sin,
with tears in their eyes and concern on their faces,
so grateful that they were born in the right places,
Non-doms with their fortunes stashed in St Tropez
can get to be heroes, but just for a day.

I'm not down on charity – it counts for a lot,
just hate the disparity between haves and have-nots,
While we get our heads shaved or run twenty miles
some celebs seem to do it to raise their profiles,
Media exposure's the name of the game
so they get on the telly and massage their fame,
For we who have nothing, we all give the most,
from city to village, from mountain to coast,
For when we pull together and all lend a hand
there's no end to what we could do in this land.

But you mean and you mighty, it's time to confess
that you'll bend any rule just to help you pay less.
So spare us your guilt-trip, you tax-dodging pricks –
and pass me your bucket, I need to be sick.

Daddy Was A Warrior

My daddy was a warrior like many at the time,
He left the farm in '34 and signed the dotted line,
And then it all went mental as the papers said it might,
And millions marched and perished to defeat the fascist Right.

From Dunkirk to Kohima and all points in between
They never really talked so much about the things they'd seen,
Destruction, devastation, broken bodies, shattered minds,
There must be a better way for poor old humankind,
Resolving to make changes for somehow they'd survived,
So many had that spirit back in 1945.

 My babies were all born with the cold war at its height
And I feared for their existence as I tucked them up at night,
The wind was blowing cold and the voice on telly said
"The way that things are going, man we're hanging by a thread!"
Creating paranoia about the other tribe
Was keeping us compliant across the great divide,
Maintaining isolation is the way they stay in power
And they make us feel the fear as we race to zero-hour
"You'd better duck and cover boy, obey and you'll survive!"
-    So much for the bullshit back in 1985.

The world is ruled by warriors yet everyone wants peace,
We need a change of management then we shall be released,
They work for mass destruction, waste billions on their wars,
Instead of buying weapons they could feed and clothe the poor,

Divide and rule's their method and it keeps them at the top,
But rising in our millions we can tell them all to STOP.
 We're here to send a message, we're here to use our voice,
Still standing at the crossroads the world can make a choice:
Not a burned-out piece of carbon in the cold and dark of space
But an earth of peace and plenty and a future we can face.
We can't betray our heritage, we daughters and we sons
– Think what mums and daddies wanted when they handed in their
guns.

Donor

I would give you an injection of confidence,
donate part of my brain to give you some sense
of your worth - immense.

Queue up at the local hall,
let them shove in a tube and syphon a pint
to give you heart, the contents of my whole bloomin' arm
to keep you from more harm.

And after my biscuit and tea,
let you choose from a shopping-list of vital parts of me.

Bone-marrow, liver, kidneys,
right arm, eye-teeth, the shirt from my back,
Whatever sacrifice it took to set you free or get you on track,
have the confidence to be who I know you to be,
the person everyone but you can clearly see.

And if I could I would give you
corneas, retina, a magic mirror to hold up every day,
help you reflect how far you have come along the way,
and show you the miracle, incredible but true,
the magic everyone can see
But you.

Extra Time

It was seventeen years since I played my last match…
I played again today.
I was the youngest of the old boys;
55 now and no hemiplaegia or balance problems for me,
No frontal lobe trauma or bits of fits
or seizures…I've been lucky.

I bossed the midfield.
Against blokes ten or more years older
I suddenly felt bolder
and was amused to hear shouts of
"Mark the young man, Get the young fella,
Get that lad, GET 'IM!"

Some of these old timers, these stroke survivors
or pals with Alzheimer's
had been very good in their time,
Made me wonder if I had been good in mine.
If you watched you would see
One with league experience, a semi-pro or two,
even a lesser-known Charlton brother,
all much better than me.
But on that playing-field we were for a spell all level.
The years rolled back
As we rolled the ball and strolled,
United by our common goal.

No losers today,

our sportsmanship and sedate pace
despite skills and tough tackles
meant we all saved face.
No silver cups or medals either
and the pitch was not exactly Wembley.
But players and fans of football are dreamers one and all,
and memories and dreams forever
Abide With Me.

In the minibus after,
some aches and pains, and a bit of wry laughter.
Lisa Stansfield sang us back to Rochdale on the radio
and as we counted down the motorway miles,
in the silences between the smiles
Some reflections of our ravaged times:
Disease, divorce or cigarettes, days in court or chronic debts,
But football gives us no regrets
and we may have recalled what great footballers -
what good and happy men -
we all had been; fifty years ago,
or twenty-five.
Or seventeen.

Five Pints Welsh

I've had a feel for English almost ever since day one,
so flexible and fluent but not - quite - my mother tongue,
For I come from a region with a history of its own

with the roots of its identity in dialect and tone,
And in my bolder moments, when drink or passion's high,
you'll hear my older accent as it soars beyond the sky,
As even in the future our traditions may still last
our voices have a beauty that can join us to our past.

We're bound to our heritage with threads so fine and pure
though they may not be visible they're audible for sure,
And all the old folks' stories of the thorny paths they walked
and long-lost former glories can be heard in how we talk.
So when the work is over and we meet to raise a glass
and foregather with our kindred we relax and drop the mask,
While some say they just don't trust the way our accents come and
go
I just say we're bang-tidy - like the tide, we ebb and flow!

So while in daily usage normal English is just fine
I love to have this choice of voice to change from time to time,
And when we feel the need to think and talk more like ourselves
I'll be three sheets Geordie, and you'll be five pints Welsh.

Food For Thought

I met her in the café while waiting for a train,
I saw her order coffee and longed to know her name,
I swiftly moved my notebook and cleared a little space,
and shyly glanced towards her as she slipped into her place.

And though the room was crowded the background slipped away, we focused on each other and I thought I heard her say

"I'll be your little cracker if you can be my cheese,
a jar of pickled gherkins can bring me to my knees,
Come with me to the deli and we'll spend our afternoons
among my baps and bagels and my cherry macaroons".

Of course I had to follow to see what I might learn,
I wondered what she swallowed to guard against heartburn,
I found that in life's banquet she's quite the omnivore,
she spreads her picnic blanket and gladly tries it all.

One thing led to another and I'm very glad to say
our gourmet feasts continue even to this very day,
Our appetites grow bigger when she's serving up the pie,
Our passion's never rationed, so our love will never die!

Gobshites

I've always been a gobshite, I've got this way with words,
is it verbal diarrhoea or just jewel-encrusted turds
of wisdom that I peddle as I swim against the stream
of popular opinion and success and all that means?

See, I've got me this affliction which, though it rarely kills
doesn't decorate my CV as a marketable skill,
Some folks say "Get a proper job, you should have made the scene
by doing something useful instead of chasing stupid dreams".

But spare a though for gobshites for we really have no choice
but to strive and scribe and scrape and try to give your hopes a
voice,
Degrees in clever writing however packed with wit
are nothing but gobshiting, when you come right down to it.

Stand and cheer for heroes who poised with pen or quill,
For Shakespeare, Blake or Dickens, Cooper-Clarke or Benny Hill,
Whitman, Wordsworth, Shelley, Robert Calvert or Pam Ayres,
authors, playwrights, poets, pissed or sober, I don't care!

Power to the workers by muscle or by brain!
we gobshites aren't just shirkers – can't you feel our pain?
We set the words on fire and make them flash and flare,
a wordsmith's still a worker, never mind the clothes and hair…

So please, be good to gobshites whenever you may meet
and please don't shout or throw things or dodge across the street;
I thank you for your patience as I bid a fond goodnight –
you're such a lovely audience – oh thank you, mine's a pint!

Hebburn

Hebburn is a place on Earth,
a sit-com in my place of birth,
Where once I roamed the building-sites
to plunder wood for bonfire night,

The wind blew raw but we felt cool,
when ships were launched they closed the schools,
With winters sharp but memories sweet,
like Franchi's fish-shop down the street,
The river roared and factories clanged
while in the teeth of gales we sang…

"The Quay School is a very good school,
It's made of bricks and plaster,
But the only thing that spoils the school
Is the baldy-heeded master!"

I loved the gentle hiss
of the little gas fire,
The soft pop of ignition and blue flames,
the white chalky fireclay filigree
strands growing hotter and glowing red
and golden as my slumbers,
Till the patterns swirled
warm and endless as dreams.

Now childhood visions help me place
and fix my heart in time and space,
More stone and flame and steel than plastic,
Hawthorn Leslie's, Bitumastic,
Reyrolle's floodlights burning bright,
factories churning day and night,
But telly programmes can't destroy
the memories of girls and boys,
Of playing out and clarts and noise,

of Mams and Dads and fairs and toys…

For life is like the bird that flew,
a truth that Bede and Cuthbert knew,
The river's song played long before
and still will sing when we're no more.

Eternal dreams, imagination,
our stolen pasts a fascination,
Saints and scholars, Vikings bold,
a timeless spell that keeps ahold
of all who bide, and all who roam…
who won't forget that this was home.

I'm On One

I'm on one, and there's no denying,
Yes I'm on one, I can feel it rising,
There's no fears of the tears I'll be crying
When I'm on one.

I'm on one, and it feels like sunshine in the morning
or the sighs of angels and the music
that I always dreamed about,
I'm on one.

I know I told you that I'd come back down to earth,
I know I promised that it really wasn't worth

all the lies and pain and all the doubt and shame
but every now and then I need to step out of the frame…
I'm on one.

I'm on one, though I might regret it in the morning,
I'm on one, I know it's bad but it's not boring,
I'm on one, and I can't forget it's what I'm here for,
do you feel the same way, are you on one?
Are you on one? Are you on one?
Let's go on one!

In Chesham Woods

Lend me your ears and give me your hand,
I need to show you something.

It's not much further now.
No further than the edge of town really,
but a more different world would be hard to imagine.
Beautiful for sure
but shaded with magic and misery,
not entirely pure. Come on,
I'll show you.

Through the tree-line in the mid-distance
we pass into an ancient darkness.
There is a clearing for resting or rituals,
further on an ornamental cave,

its hermit long-departed, the haunt
of witches and drinkers and all beings spiritual.

Along the bluebell path I roamed in dreams
and recognised the landscape
that inspired Richmal's ruffians,
Tousle-haired adventures,
William and young Outlaws.

We pass a blackthorn hedge planted by me in better days
and cross two bridges I built with timeworn timber
and nails pin-bright, yearning for my hammer,
And these
yes these bloody hands.

Finally we sit at the side of Five Acre Meadow
and in the long grass glory and mocking sunshine
flood her funeral together with not enough wine
to stop me wishing she was here
Instead of you.

Irwell Street (Falling Mortar)

They're pulling down Irwell Street nick,
but without wrecking balls or dynamite,
They're doing it by hand, with shovels and picks,
because of all the asbestos.
I would have said "brick-by-brick"
but there's hardly a brick in it;
It's all breeze-block and concrete and smoked glass.
Most people say it had no class
but then some don't see with their imaginations.
Like Marineville or Tracy Island, I saw a futuristic H.Q.
Space City for the seventies or some other-worldy sci-fi nation.

I say it had…style; and a jarring, out-of-context,
juxtaposed, dystopian drama.
Others immune to this artistic charmer,
prefer to see virtue in filthy chimneys,
give listed to status to any old shit that's dark or satanic.
It reminded me of something by the great Frank Lloyd Wright,
But in this, as in life, I sometimes sing a lonely song –
My friends all say it's more like Frank Lloyd Wrong.

Lifeline

Run down the platform, slam shut the battered, blue steel door,
the diesel engine gives a gutteral roar,
my head on the window brings a rhythmic, mechanical comfort,
And I'm away!

Away from the hard work and heartache,
away from the winter and the dark, wet west,
Through the big tunnel towards the light at the end,

leaving all the doubt and despair,
Leaving it all behind.

Beyond the grim grey gritstone, the rainwashed
black slate and choking chimneys
will soon be just memories.
Head on window, wheels on rail, relentless rhythm repeats without fail,
Coming back home, coming back home.

I'm heading for houses where the sun rises,
no longer a dirty old part of the city, a place we had to get out of.
Now the land waves wheat-yellow its welcome
beneath giant ice-blue skies.
Thin clouds up aheight like wave patterns
swept by the bitter clean north-easterlies
straight off the sea, just like wor ancestors, man,
Straight off the sea.

This is the land of Northumbrian and Dane.
I know how you talk, I know how you think,
I know how you dream and laugh and drink.
From Wharfe to Tweed anywhere would do,
but tonight, Sweet City, it had to be you.

Me voice is changing with every sip from the can,
with every passing village and town.
Garforth, Micklefield, flat fields, red roofs;
Church Fenton, Ulleskelf, yew trees stand sentinel
like a ghostly Roman legion,

not the last lost souls of this harmed and harried region,
(It's aalreet, man, it's me, lerriz through!)
Copmanthorpe left, Acaster right,
under the bridge now your spires are in sight.

I leave the crowded station for a stroll down ancient streets,
pause for a read of the Evening Press, a pint or two in peace.
An iron cord, a lifeline train, has brought me back to Earth,
to a place where no-one knows my name but I can feel my worth.

Or was it that much stronger tie?
The spell of love and recklessness
no duty can defy?

Motormouth

You're not a bad guy but you're obviously high,
Your face is going red and there's that look in your eyes
that I've seen before when you start slamming doors
and you're talking too fast, see I think I know the score,
You made a valid point thirty seconds ago,
we could have a conversation if you talked more slow,
Three hundred words a minute, I think I've reached my limit,
there's a whirlpool in your brain and I think I'm falling in it,
It's a hundred things and a thousand others,
I'm coming up for air because I'm feeling kind of smothered,
You've the arrogance of youth but you wrap it in untruths,
silence can be golden and now you're the living proof,

The basis of your mind race is what I find absurd,
tying me in knots, you think I'm hanging on your words,
You hardly pause for breath when you're going on and on,
I think I'm going deaf and my patience has gone,
Getting off your face is the way you cope,
getting out of this place is now my only hope
So for now I'll say goodbye, we'll find another date,
I'll try again tomorrow when your head's a bit straighter,
(Top one, nice one, sorted, later!)

One Of Those Days

It was one of those days with an awkward feel,
when the town looks dirty and down-at-heel,
And you're on the drink but you need a meal,
it was just a-one of those days.

Filthy windows and dusty shoes,
ragged flowers and the summertime blues,
Same old shit in the Evening News,
it was just one of those days.

Wrapped up tight but you feel so cold,
all you see is rust where there once was gold,
Your hair needs cutting and you're looking old,
it was just one of those days.

You hate to smoke but you want a fag,

blossom in the trees was just carrier bags,
Love's young dream was just a shag,
it was just one of those days.

That pig in a vote wasn't what it seemed,
I'm keeping a grip to suppress the scream,
A minutes silence for my broken dream,
it was just one of those days.

And I swear right now, if I had my way,
I would pass a law to turn night to day,
And make brilliant dreams from Tory grey,
and we'd have no more of these days;
Yes, we'd have no more of these days.

Our Children (And Me)

There was always a bee in your bonnet, Blood in your guts, and a
dark flame burned in your eyes. After all that you'd been through and
what had been through you, Nobody should be surprised.
The way we look, the set of face, There are reasons sometimes if
even hard to trace, We none of us can help it deep down. Battered
from pillar to pillow to pillock to duvet of betrayal and disbelief,
Innocence stolen by a treacherous thief, How many abused have to
falter and fail, How few abusers go to jail?
I got the gist of it, we made a good fist of it and joined together in the
fight, At first side-by-side. But exhausted eventually by the battles

found enemies closer to home instead. There'd never be a problem, we jokingly said, If we could live our whole lives in this lovely bed. We moved on. And now you're gone and for me the afternoon shadows are growing long. And sometimes and old picture or the catch of a song will poleaxe me, knock me off my feet. Your memory is forever dappled, it needs both sunshine and shade to be complete.

So while I'll never forget all the venom and spite, the sorrow and anger, the sulphur and shite, I may pick up a fragment you once wrote and be gripped by the throat by a mark you made with a ball-point pen that takes me back to our youth, I can see living proof, The echoing worth of our shared mirth.

My life is as complete as the little circle above your letter "i", as crazily on the slide as the gentle glide of the tail of your "g".

While in the lengthening afternoon I still make the tea; As you made your mark on our children and me.

Palestine

There was, or there was not, in the oldness of time,
A land that some today refuse to find.

Misunderstood, mistaken, misplaced, disgraced,
All but completely taken,
by powers that be maligned, forsaken.

A place with grudged presence
as much by its absence defined,
To some a vague archaic insult –
"Philistine" –
or like Schrodinger's Cat,
both there and yet not there at the same time.

Identity shifting
like the sands of shores Levantine,
Now forcibly removed by blood and iron,
the scarcely believable hand of Zion.
Consciousness rudely awoken
by lives and families broken,
land and livelihoods stolen,
Guns, barbed wire and the wrong kind of shell,
The ones you can hear without putting them
to your yearning, listening ear.

But come with me and walk the sand
with eyes closed against the outraged land,
Look within to feel and see

a dream of freedom yet to be,
For dreams are the grandparents
of reality.

From West Bank and Gaza to far-off Chile's sea and sky,
the seashell whispers grow loud and multiply.
Twelve million grains of sand borne by the breeze
Fly over barriers like scattered refugees,
find hollows in the walls of time,
points of contact, ill-defined,
Caves of the familiar.

If I hadn't seen such riches I could live with being poor,
If I didn't have the key I wouldn't care about the door,
But held in house or heart or hand,
the key will guide us home once more.

There was, or there will be, in the fullness of time,
Beyond the war

Palestine.

Public Service

I can't make your dinner, I can't mend your car,
can't sell you insurance or tune your guitar,
Can't plaster your ceiling or build your extension ,
my skills on computers don't warrant a mention,
Don't make flat-screen tellies or pasteurise milk,
I don't tailor jackets of satin or silk,
I don't labour no more on a factory floor,
and I don't dig for coal or hammer or saw,
I don't make ANYTHING, and I'm not self-employed,
I'm the kind of worker who gets the media annoyed,
And they look down on us, like we should be ashamed
(and they want everybody to feel just the same).

They cut services and wages and privatise
till we can't afford stuff that the go-getters buy,
In our third-hand cars and our ten quid shoes
in our tiny houses with our bargain booze,
(Though more often than not it's enforced sobriety
we're standing outside this consumer society),
It's a different world - but I ask is it real?
or just an illusion like Deal Or No Deal?
And believe me, it gives me no pleasure to say
though you may not have seen us, you'll need us one day.

For we are the people who'll hold your hand
and talk about ways to look after your Mam,
Or reach out to help when your health has all gone
and try to build bridges when life has gone wrong.

We nurse and we counsel, we care and we teach,
we're emotional therapists who keep you in reach,
When fate has conspired to kick you in the teeth
we're the folk who can stop you from sinking beneath,
Our care's a reminder when cursing your lot
of the value of things that you almost forgot.

To hell with fat pensions and investment plans,
Those dodgy remortgage or buy-to-rent scams,
Obsessive compulsion will lead to a fall,
excessive consumption is killing us all.

So you keep your dollars, and I'll keep my soul;
our poor, public service is more precious than gold.

Shipping Container

I want to live in a shipping container, that would be like heaven for
me,
No mortgage crap and no retainers, no council tax or agents fees,
No excess space, my green sustainer will show the world a better
way,
And if I get some nasty neighbours I'll load the truck and just drive
away.

I want to live in a shipping container, take my pick of where to park
it,
Dreaming of my next back-garden, city, seaside, moor or market,
Don't need room for sprawling mansions, greed for land just can't go
on,
I've no use for wild expansion when I'm nine feet square by forty
long.

The world could live in shipping containers, customise them as we
please,
No debt, no banks and no disclaimers in self-sufficient societies,
Share the space and share the leisure, smash the chains of slavery,
They won't own us, what a pleasure! Then our children can be
FREE!

Strings

Your strings have been cut.
And now some say you swan and strut
about, flitting from place to place
like a butterfly, pleasure-seeking, individual…

They should talk. Still tied up
and dancing like puppets,
Jumping and jiving at the merest finger's twitch.
they envy your freedom,
think you a reckless bitch for your vain folly
while they are still in dishonest thrall
for money and men, lying on their backs
and through their teeth for dirty lolly.

Your strings have been cut.
So why are they so surprised
when the first thing you do is fly away,
like a kite careering crazily high?

Later you will come down
and dare to learn, unaided,
freely and unfettered to walk.
They should dare.
They should talk.

The Bride Wore Blue

The bride wore blue to match her tattoos
and the groom was a staggering wreck,
With his broken nose and his wilted rose
and the love-bites all over his neck,
The hall was bare, just tables and chairs,
and the snow blew in under the door,
We were there six hours and the beer was sour
and the cake ended up on the floor.

The speeches were short then a few of them fought
while the in-laws sneaked off to the pub
The groom was so pissed, swung a punch but he missed
and he landed face-down in the grub,
A gaggle of schoolies, tanked-up and unruly,
were smoking and cursing and snogging,
Then a gran, unashamed, yelled "Sod this for a game,
is there anyone else coming dogging?"

I've never spent so much time casting pearls before swine,
every one was a pain in the neck,
Though I'd worked my balls off they then capped it all off
by paying not cash but by cheque.
The bride wore blue to match her tattoos,
but the gig was worth more than the wage,
For this night of frustration was ideal preparation
for my glamorous life on the stage.

The Brown Bear

The Brown Bear has been refurbished, but not ruined.
Spruced up and burnished, this noble bruin
no longer a pit is safe in the city
and lively with Saturday afternoon chatter.
The fire crackles and the crack and patter
glow warmer by the hour.

I'm sitting comfortably
where septuagenarian Sheffielders sip Sam Smith's
from silver tankards,
getting slowly wankered.
A group of students saunters past,
eery ghosts of me and friends thirty years ago,
but the haunting does not last,
and the evening's only just begun.

Just one more pint
and like the pub, I'm restored.
Not nearly pissed, once more the optimist
I was at twenty-one.

The Skipton Bus

Another ruined Sunday,
the dread of Monday school
and, later, work

casting their grim shadows over one seventh
of our lives.
The day of the Lord,
we servants obeying the ordered
and regimented routines and rules,
We are reminded with timetable regularity
about our station as the bus pulls in
to take us home.

Morning's thoughts of God, hopes of heaven
dissolved by seven in the evening's gathering gloom.
Tomorrow machines will grind and roar,
teachers will sneer and bore
as adults and children bow once more
to the blackboard wall or factory floor,
bones to be chewed by the system's ever-hungry maw.

From high street market heat and hustle
to cooling castle courtyard or the clink of bone china
The family retreats and takes seats,
with one or two whispered, wistful dreams that

"One of these days
we won't need a return ticket,
we'll stay here, wouldn't that be lovely?
Lovely, yes, lovely…"
But this is for now no transport of delight,
we've had a great day but now it's Sunday night…
and we head south,
pulled by the thirty mile elastic, invisible but strong,

That drags us away from temptation
but delivers us back to evil;
To those who own us,
to where we belong.

The Two Tubs

This town was built on a rock.
The reason we're here is the forty-foot drop
on the north side, masked these days by the bypass.
As thousands pass by daily
without a second thought
for iron-age settlers or a medieval fort.

There was once a reason why
primitive travellers or nomadic tribes
paused for a while, felt safe to stop,
lit fires, sang and drank and danced till they dropped.

Centuries later near the very same spot
someone sawed a barrel in half and nailed the two bits
to the wall of the Tubs.

And today, like the barrels, this is a pub of two halves.
Modern and ancient, no need for replacement,
the cellar not so much a basement
as a medieval catacomb,
of hewn stone like a family tomb.

as cold and calm as Dracula's front room!

Anomalies like a stone-mullioned window six feet under
who needs an underground window, you wonder?
Give weight to the rumours of underground tunnels,
connections to other underworlds in this town,
secret doors, stone-flagged floors, not haunts of the devil
may just show that the deep and dark were once street-level.

Our name itself is rare – In ancient Anglian
"dative after lost preposition" has softened our inflection,
it's why we're "Bury" and not "Burg"…
Something always happening, not just some Manc suburb,
still standing but never standing still,
it's a crossroads, a meeting-point, twixt West and East a junction,
A place for public and private functions,
full of northern fun and frenzy and goings-on and gumption.

So after working week or heavy mile,
when heart or head make it hard to smile,
Or division of your joy demands you celebrate in style,
like the ancients, pause for a while.

Feel safe to stop near fires, fulfil desires,
a snog in secret in the snug,
come in, love, it's a shop!
Sing, and drink, and dance till you drop!

Three Limericks

There once was a poet called Chris
who enjoyed going out on the piss,
Justified each libation
as it gave inspiration –
A logic that's hard to resist.

This government, smarmy and smooth,
talk bullshit they never can prove,
But if you want to try
you can tell when they lie –
It's whenever you see their lips move.

Some serious colleagues of mine
deplore any poem that rhymes,
They say rhyming is worse
than their clever free verse,
But I don't understand their point, myself…

Men Wearing Ties

Beware, beware the men wearing ties,
the smooth-talking, suit-wearing women,
plastic-tongued, time-serving careerists,
Bourgeois and fascist, aggressive and passive,
bully boys and tyrants.

They joined the party as a cynical decision
and with perfect precision never hear the derision
as they mooch and schmooze their way to the top,
Think nothing can stop their chosen jobsworthy path,
despite the party members or others who might laugh,
or say their policies are crap!
And they really belong in another party with a more bitter flavour.
They laugh in your face, think that they know your place,
don't you realise, plebs, that they're doing you a favour?

Oh yes, mister haircut and suit, Ms boorish and brute,
Mister soundbite and gobshite, they've never been deep,
I can see they're just creeps.
I've got no time for cowards and traitors,
I can spot those Tory infiltrators
from a hundred yards in a red-mist fog,
with one good eye and my National Health gogs.

For the Right has a thousand lies
and the high and mighty wear flashy ties
and try to ignore all the cries and the sighs
of all of us who they so despise,
I can see them for miles, and miles, and miles –
They're the bastards on telly who always wear ties.

Under My Skin

You're under my skin like a nasty rash.
like an expired cheque I forgot to cash,
As out of reach as my hidden stash,
you're in so deep a needle can't scratch,
My best defence was just no match,
what made me think I was such a catch?
And now, you're under my skin.

You're in my head though we're far apart,
like a happy ending without a start,
Like Manchester but without the tart,
my beaten body doesn't bear a mark,
My soul's intact but when it comes to my heart
you're the beating, mistreating, cheating part,
Here beneath my skin

Constant craving's getting on my nerves,
I'll play it straight round your deadly curves,
An empty dream is less than I deserve,
booting the brakes, giving you a swerve,
Not seduced, just reduced like you're some kind of perv,
and whatever your thang is It sure isn't lurrve,
So where do I begin?

You tugged my string just for something to do,
an empty promise that never came true,
A bubble that burst the more you blew,

whatever happened to a good, honest screw?
This is my lightbulb moment, so un-screw you,
Don't want you under my skin.

After due contemplation it's my consideration
that you need a vacation far away from temptation
here's a lift to the station, you can make a migration
to a far constellation or desolate nation,
spend the rest of creation in some mute meditation,
unfulfilled masturbation or some other damnation…

But still, you'll be under my skin,
Yes, I've got you under my skin.

Up To Twelve

Don't need your fancy instruments, no strings that cost ten grand,
we just have a mighty rhythm and it echoes through the land,
It's the hammer of the shipyard, the weaving shed's loud call,
the power-press on sheets of steel, the noise that moves us all,
The bass is like a heartbeat, it makes my pulses race,
the drums fire up the engines on our journey into space,
We're dancing in a vortex at the edges of your mind,
a vision of eternity one heartbeart at a time.

Some say we're three-chord wonders, but I say that's not true,
three chords are much too fancy, we get by with two,
So good luck with your boy-bands and your so-called R&B,

Pop Factor and X-Idol, it's all the same to me,
Those pseudo-intellectuals from the self-styled upper-class,
they wouldn't know excitement if it bit them on the arse,
Just give me drums and passion, some bass and lead guitars,
play it fast and crank it up and point me at the stars!

Still, in the end it's your choice – you've got to please yourselves –
But here's the way we like it, Baby – these amps go up to twelve.

We'll Meet Again

We'll meet again, don't know where, don't know when,
don't know IF.
We've lost our people's finest gift,
the instinct to care for each other.
Instead of comrades, sisters, brothers we see a churning mass,
a seething swarming seascape of thieves and threats
about to attack.
We condemn and convict, to fill the void left
by the compassion we've been taught to lack.

Sent over the top by oppression,
whistleblown, regulated and sanctioned into depression,
Regimented, derided, divided and ruled,
the generals think they have us fooled,
gathering around to watch and jeer our dogfights.
Our orders are given, instructions on screens
or mailed daily, stamped viciously in black and white,

who to fear today, who to hate today, who to fight.
But always despite the names that change
the enemy somehow remains the same –
It's the people over there, that lot, the others…it's us against them.

Shell-shocked and bruised, some of us have begun to refuse,
meeting in No-Man's Land for a Christmas truce.

We come together, swap family photos,
don't rain venom and blows on each other's heads,
but kick a football instead.
We see faces, smiles, and the faint flicker of humanity
behind bloodshot, bayonet eyes.
We see it's our tormentors we must learn to despise.

United by our true class, peace may break out
and we may break through at last.
When, in the open, on the streets, with open hands and hearts,
However long it takes, we'll meet again, my friends…
And we can make a start.

The Warmth

And now I'm getting The Warmth. Thank the gods or whatever you
want for The Warmth, the glow, the feeling, the flow, Contentment at
last. I've worked so hard, Played most if not every card And here I
am, I feel it, this thing I feel. It's true, it's vital, it's Real.
Now I remember why I do what I do, Why you might not understand,
Alone but reaching out to you. Where anywhere I am can be

absolutely any land or space, or time, or colour, or mood... The warmth is good, the warmth is good.

All day there's been that rarity, a February light in the sky, A Radar Love of days gone by and I have been in Amsterdam or Haarlem every bit as much as I have been here. My friend wrote "Achttien honderd uurs, en het is nog licht in het westen van het land!" You might think it's Double Dutch but I know you'll understand when I tell you all it means is Spring is on the way.

In Haarlem, Hexham, Heptonstall or anywhere on the way, or a thousand other places I thought of you all today, As I will tomorrow, forever and yesterday.

For the sun has thawed the northern wastes and kissed the frozen, northern places and the withered, nithered northern faces of the now-delivered northern races. So I will raise my glass and sing my song - the winter's gone! And The Warmth...The Warmth is good.

When We Don't Do What We're Told

Forget Magna Carta - give me Peasants' Revolt!
From the People's Charter to when women got the vote,
From the Dorset Martyrs in the days of old,
Things get better when we don't do what we're told!
From free education to sharing out the wealth
To old age pensions and the National Health,
Our hard-won achievements were not built in a day,
But now the greedy bosses want to take them all away. In the
struggle for survival and improvements for the poor
We may lose many battles but still can win the war,
Show the blasted rulers that we won't be bought and sold –
Things get better when we don't do what we're told.
So solidly together, be proud and brave and bold,
Things get better when we don't do what we're told,
We can seize the hour when we don't do what we're told,
VICTORY IS OURS,
WHEN
WE
DON'T
DO
WHAT
WE'RE
TOLD